Financial Mindfulness

Journal

A tool for money management and life skills

This journal is meant to explore our finances in a way that allows for mindful choices. We can only make so much money, which means it is a limited resource. Our ability to make money depends on our health, our education, our mental and physical skills, and the job market.

Since we can only make so much of it, if we want to reach our financial life goals we will need to be careful with each dollar that we earn. Having a budget with a line item for each expense we have, for both needs and wants, will help us achieve our goals.

Your journal will allow you to determine needs from wants, set personal and professional money goals, and move forward with intention being mindful of each dollar you earn.

Still not sure where to begin? Money Lit offers educational resources and workshops to help you develop your money life skills. If you are interested in more information on our **budgeting or investment workshops,** or for more supplemental classes and materials: **email us at: MoneyLitLearning@gmail.com** or check us out on social media and send us a message there. We also offer Trading Trackers for an introduction into investing if you want to learn how to make your money work for you.

Happy money managing!

Copyright © 2022 by Stephanie D. Pyke

All rights reserved. No part of this book may be reproduced or used in any manner without written permission of the copyright owner except for the use of quotations in a book review. For more information, address: MoneyLitLearning@gmail.com
FIRST EDITION

My Vision Board

Physical:	Mental:	Spiritual:	Financial:

Things to try:

- _____
- _____
- _____
- _____
- _____

Itentions this year:

Wants & Needs

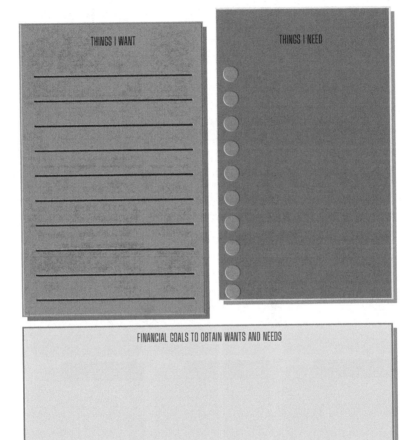

THINGS I WANT

THINGS I NEED

FINANCIAL GOALS TO OBTAIN WANTS AND NEEDS

NEEDS ARE THE THINGS THAT WE REQUIRE TO LIVE (WATER, AIR, FOOD). WE BUDGET AND PAY FOR THESE THINGS FIRST. WANTS ARE THE THINGS WE WOULD LIKE TO HAVE BUT COULD DO WITHOUT IF WE NEED TO BE MORE MINDFUL OF SAVING OR INVESTING.

Yearly Investing Planner

JANUARY GOAL	FEBRUARY GOAL	MARCH GOAL
APRIL GOAL	MAY GOAL	JUNE GOAL
JULY GOAL	AUGUST GOAL	SEPTEMBER GOAL
OCTOBER GOAL	NOVEMBER GOAL	DECEMBER GOAL

WHY INVEST? MONEY IS A LIMITED RESOURCE. INVESTING MAKES YOUR HARD EARNED RESOURCE WORK FOR YOU.

DEBT PAYMENT
TRACKER

Min. Payment:												Total Payment:		

Month												Amount	Bill
1	2	3	4	5	6	7	8	9	10	11	12		

Important

SUBSCRIPTIONS
TRACKER

What subscriptions do you have? Go through your bank/credit card statements and write them all here. Keep track. Pay attention to which ones you don't use anymore. Cancel them. Only keep what you are using. Money is a limited resource, be mindful of where yours is going.

Month												Amount	Subscription
1	2	3	4	5	6	7	8	9	10	11	12		

Important

Weekly Meal Planner

Grocery List

Breakfast	Lunch	Dinner	Snacks
mon			
tue			
wed			
thu			
fri			
sat			
sun			

Quarterly Budget Planner

Jan, Feb, March _____

INCOME STREAMS

SOURCE	AFTER TAX	ACTUAL	DIFFERENCES
Income			
Side Hustles			
Business			
Others			

FIXED AND VARIABLE EXPENSES

EXPENSES	CURRENT MONTHLY COST	ADJUSTMENTS	MONTHLY DUE DATE
HOUSEHOLD			
RENT/MORTGAGE			
ELECTRIC/GAS/OIL/PROPANE			
WATER/SEWER/SEPTIC/GARBAGE			
RENTER/HOME OWNER INS			
HOME MAINTENANCE			
CAR/MAINTENANCE			
CAR LOAN			
CAR INSURANCE			
CAR MAINTENANCE			
GROCERIES			
FOOD			
HOUSEHOLD ITEMS			
ENTERTAINMENT			
WEEKEND FUN			
WEEKDAY FUN			

Quarterly Budget Planner

HAIR/NAILS			
LAUNDRY			
LUNCH OUT			
PARKING			
GYM/HEALTH CLUB MEMBERSHIP			
INTERNET/CABLE			
STREAMING SUBSCRIPTIONS			
STUDENT LOANS			
TAXES (SELF-EMPLOYED)			
SPORTS/ACTIVITIES			

EXPENSES	CURRENT MONTHLY COST	ADJUSTMENTS	MONTHLY DUE DATE
CHILD CARE			
CLOTHING			
VACATION/TRAVEL			
PROFESSIONAL MEMBERSHIPS			
RX/DR. COPAYS/DENTAL			
HOLIDAYS/BIRTHDAYS			
DEBTS:			

SAVINGS

	TOTAL SAVINGS
Total Income (After Tax)	
Total Fixed Expenses	
Total Variable Expenses	
Savings - Income + Expenses	

THINGS I
CAN CONTROL

Ex. My Mood

Write in the things you **CAN** control in your life. Focus on those things today. Perspective is everything.

My MONTHLY ✳ PLAN

January:
_____

To do list

_____

_____

_____

_____

_____

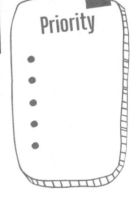

Morning Routine

Priority

- •
- •
- •
- •
- •

Notes

I love my self

HABIT TRACKER

Name _____
Year _____
Month _____

Habit   _____
Goal   _____
Done   _____
Reward   _____

Sun	Mon	Tue	Wed	Thu	Fri	Sat
☐	☐	☐	☐	☐	☐	☐
☐	☐	☐	☐	☐	☐	☐
☐	☐	☐	☐	☐	☐	☐
☐	☐	☐	☐	☐	☐	☐

Habit   _____
Goal   _____
Done   _____
Reward   _____

Sun	Mon	Tue	Wed	Thu	Fri	Sat
☐	☐	☐	☐	☐	☐	☐
☐	☐	☐	☐	☐	☐	☐
☐	☐	☐	☐	☐	☐	☐
☐	☐	☐	☐	☐	☐	☐

Habit   _____
Goal   _____
Done   _____
Reward   _____

Sun	Mon	Tue	Wed	Thu	Fri	Sat
☐	☐	☐	☐	☐	☐	☐
☐	☐	☐	☐	☐	☐	☐
☐	☐	☐	☐	☐	☐	☐
☐	☐	☐	☐	☐	☐	☐

Habit   _____
Goal   _____
Done   _____
Reward   _____

Sun	Mon	Tue	Wed	Thu	Fri	Sat
☐	☐	☐	☐	☐	☐	☐
☐	☐	☐	☐	☐	☐	☐
☐	☐	☐	☐	☐	☐	☐
☐	☐	☐	☐	☐	☐	☐

My Monthly Brain Dump List

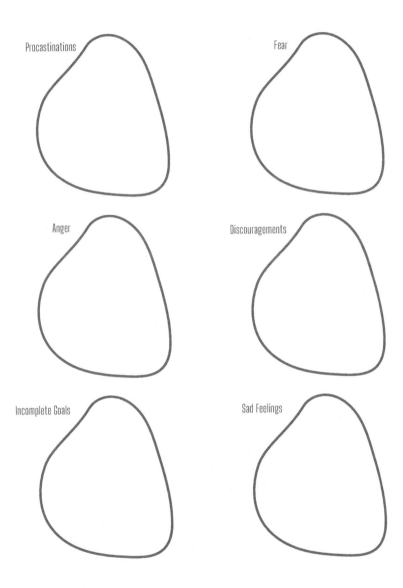

Procastinations

Fear

Anger

Discouragements

Incomplete Goals

Sad Feelings

5 Minute Weekly Journaling

_____

_____

_____

_____

_____

_____

_____

_____

_____

_____

_____

_____

_____

_____

_____

_____

_____

_____

5 Minute Weekly
Journaling

---

5 Minute Weekly Journaling

---

5 Minute Weekly
Journaling

_____
_____
_____
_____
_____
_____
_____
_____
_____
_____
_____
_____
_____
_____
_____
_____

I
AM
GRATEFUL
FOR

Ex. Sunshine

My MONTHLY ✳
PLAN

February:
_____

To do list

_____
_____
_____
_____
_____

Morning Routine

Priority

- •
- •
- •
- •
- •

Notes

I love my self

HABIT TRACKER

Name _____
Year _____
Month _____

Habit _____
Goal _____
Done _____
Reward _____

Sun	Mon	Tue	Wed	Thu	Fri	Sat
☐	☐	☐	☐	☐	☐	☐
☐	☐	☐	☐	☐	☐	☐
☐	☐	☐	☐	☐	☐	☐
☐	☐	☐	☐	☐	☐	☐

Habit _____
Goal _____
Done _____
Reward _____

Sun	Mon	Tue	Wed	Thu	Fri	Sat
☐	☐	☐	☐	☐	☐	☐
☐	☐	☐	☐	☐	☐	☐
☐	☐	☐	☐	☐	☐	☐
☐	☐	☐	☐	☐	☐	☐

Habit _____
Goal _____
Done _____
Reward _____

Sun	Mon	Tue	Wed	Thu	Fri	Sat
☐	☐	☐	☐	☐	☐	☐
☐	☐	☐	☐	☐	☐	☐
☐	☐	☐	☐	☐	☐	☐
☐	☐	☐	☐	☐	☐	☐

Habit _____
Goal _____
Done _____
Reward _____

Sun	Mon	Tue	Wed	Thu	Fri	Sat
☐	☐	☐	☐	☐	☐	☐
☐	☐	☐	☐	☐	☐	☐
☐	☐	☐	☐	☐	☐	☐
☐	☐	☐	☐	☐	☐	☐

My Monthly Brain Dump List

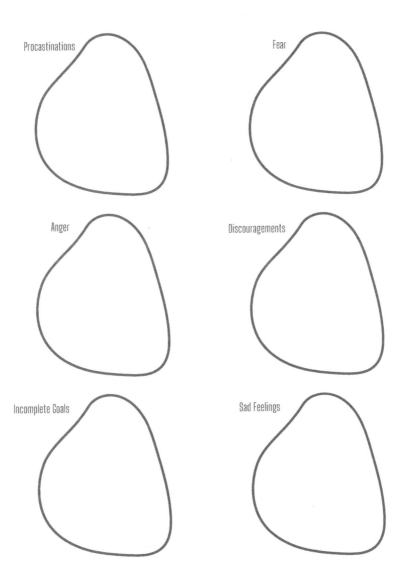

Procastinations

Fear

Anger

Discouragements

Incomplete Goals

Sad Feelings

5 Minute Weekly
Journaling

_____
_____
_____
_____
_____
_____
_____
_____
_____
_____
_____
_____
_____
_____
_____
_____
_____

5 Minute Weekly
Journaling

_____

_____

_____

_____

_____

_____

_____

_____

_____

_____

_____

_____

_____

_____

_____

_____

5 Minute Weekly
Journaling

_____

_____

_____

_____

_____

_____

_____

_____

_____

_____

_____

_____

_____

_____

_____

5 Minute Weekly Journaling

_____

_____

_____

_____

_____

_____

_____

_____

_____

_____

_____

_____

_____

_____

BOOK LIST TO READ

LIST	AUTHOR	RATING	READ
		☆☆☆☆☆	☐
		☆☆☆☆☆	☐
		☆☆☆☆☆	☐
		☆☆☆☆☆	☐
		☆☆☆☆☆	☐
		☆☆☆☆☆	☐
		☆☆☆☆☆	☐
		☆☆☆☆☆	☐
		☆☆☆☆☆	☐
		☆☆☆☆☆	☐
		☆☆☆☆☆	☐
		☆☆☆☆☆	☐
		☆☆☆☆☆	☐
		☆☆☆☆☆	☐
		☆☆☆☆☆	☐
		☆☆☆☆☆	☐
		☆☆☆☆☆	☐
		☆☆☆☆☆	☐
		☆☆☆☆☆	☐
		☆☆☆☆☆	☐
		☆☆☆☆☆	☐

NOTES

My MONTHLY ✳ PLAN

March:
_____

To do list

_____

_____

_____

_____

_____

Morning Routine

Priority

- •
- •
- •
- •
- •

Notes

I love my self

HABIT TRACKER

Name _____
Year _____
Month _____

Habit _____
Goal _____
Done _____
Reward _____

Sun	Mon	Tue	Wed	Thu	Fri	Sat
☐	☐	☐	☐	☐	☐	☐
☐	☐	☐	☐	☐	☐	☐
☐	☐	☐	☐	☐	☐	☐

Habit _____
Goal _____
Done _____
Reward _____

Sun	Mon	Tue	Wed	Thu	Fri	Sat
☐	☐	☐	☐	☐	☐	☐
☐	☐	☐	☐	☐	☐	☐
☐	☐	☐	☐	☐	☐	☐
☐	☐	☐	☐	☐	☐	☐

Habit _____
Goal _____
Done _____
Reward _____

Sun	Mon	Tue	Wed	Thu	Fri	Sat
☐	☐	☐	☐	☐	☐	☐
☐	☐	☐	☐	☐	☐	☐
☐	☐	☐	☐	☐	☐	☐
☐	☐	☐	☐	☐	☐	☐

Habit _____
Goal _____
Done _____
Reward _____

Sun	Mon	Tue	Wed	Thu	Fri	Sat
☐	☐	☐	☐	☐	☐	☐
☐	☐	☐	☐	☐	☐	☐
☐	☐	☐	☐	☐	☐	☐
☐	☐	☐	☐	☐	☐	☐

My Monthly Brain Dump List

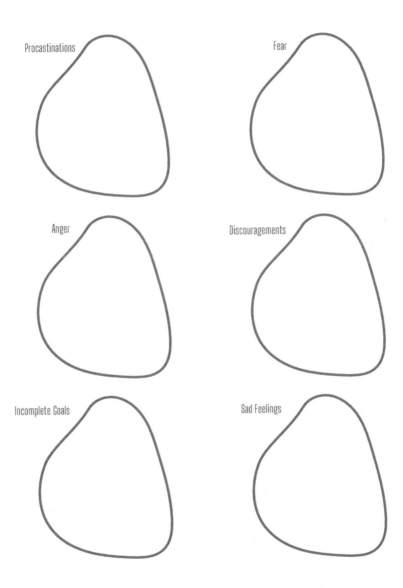

Procastinations

Fear

Anger

Discouragements

Incomplete Goals

Sad Feelings

5 Minute Weekly
Journaling

_____
_____
_____
_____
_____
_____
_____
_____
_____
_____
_____
_____
_____
_____
_____
_____

5 Minute Weekly
Journaling

_____

_____

_____

_____

_____

_____

_____

_____

_____

_____

_____

_____

_____

_____

_____

_____

_____

5 Minute Weekly Journaling

_____

_____

_____

_____

_____

_____

_____

_____

_____

_____

_____

_____

_____

_____

_____

_____

_____

5 Minute Weekly
Journaling

_____
_____
_____
_____
_____
_____
_____
_____
_____
_____
_____
_____
_____
_____
_____
_____

Quarterly Budget Planner

April, May, June _____

INCOME STREAMS

SOURCE	AFTER TAX	ACTUAL	DIFFERENCES
Income			
Side Hustles			
Business			
Others			

FIXED AND VARIABLE EXPENSES

EXPENSES	CURRENT MONTHLY COST	ADJUSTMENTS	MONTHLY DUE DATE
HOUSEHOLD			
RENT/MORTGAGE			
ELECTRIC/GAS/OIL/PROPANE			
WATER/SEWER/SEPTIC/GARBAGE			
RENTER/HOME OWNER INS			
HOME MAINTENANCE			
CAR/MAINTENANCE			
CAR LOAN			
CAR INSURANCE			
CAR MAINTENANCE			
GROCERIES			
FOOD			
HOUSEHOLD ITEMS			
ENTERTAINMENT			
WEEKEND FUN			
WEEKDAY FUN			

Quarterly Budget Planner

HAIR/NAILS			
LAUNDRY			
LUNCH OUT			
PARKING			
GYM/HEALTH CLUB MEMBERSHIP			

INTERNET/CABLE			
STREAMING SUBSCRIPTIONS			
STUDENT LOANS			
TAXES (SELF-EMPLOYED)			
SPORTS/ACTIVITIES			

EXPENSES	CURRENT MONTHLY COST	ADJUSTMENTS	MONTHLY DUE DATE
CHILD CARE			
CLOTHING			
VACATION/TRAVEL			
PROFESSIONAL MEMBERSHIPS			
RX/DR. COPAYS/DENTAL			
HOLIDAYS/BIRTHDAYS			
DEBTS:			

SAVINGS

	TOTAL SAVINGS
Total Income (After Tax)	
Total Fixed Expenses	
Total Variable Expenses	
Savings - Income + Expenses	

Money
Saving Plan

What am I saving for:

_____

$ ....
$ ....
$ ....
$ ....
$ ....
$ ....
$ ....
$ ....
$ ....
$ ....

Instructions:
1. Write in your money goal amounts next to the $.
2. Color between the lines as you reach your goal

My MONTHLY ✳ **PLAN**

April: _____

To do list

_____
_____
_____
_____
_____

Morning Routine

Priority

Notes

I love my self

HABIT TRACKER

Name _____
Year _____
Month _____

Sun	Mon	Tue	Wed	Thu	Fri	Sat

Habit _____
Goal _____
Done _____
Reward _____

Sun	Mon	Tue	Wed	Thu	Fri	Sat

Habit _____
Goal _____
Done _____
Reward _____

Sun	Mon	Tue	Wed	Thu	Fri	Sat

Habit _____
Goal _____
Done _____
Reward _____

Sun	Mon	Tue	Wed	Thu	Fri	Sat

Habit _____
Goal _____
Done _____
Reward _____

My Monthly Brain Dump List

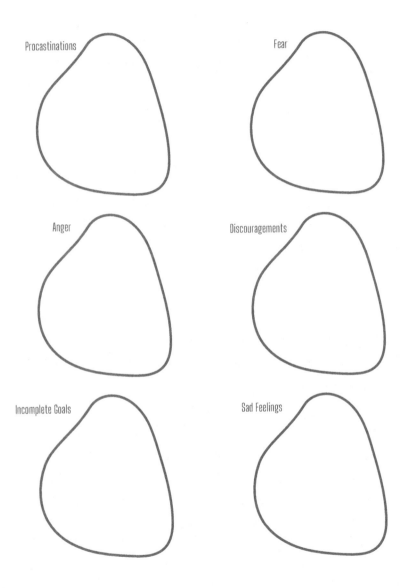

Procastinations

Fear

Anger

Discouragements

Incomplete Goals

Sad Feelings

5 Minute Weekly
Journaling

_____

_____

_____

_____

_____

_____

_____

_____

_____

_____

_____

_____

_____

_____

5 Minute Weekly
Journaling

_____

_____

_____

_____

_____

_____

_____

_____

_____

_____

_____

_____

_____

_____

_____

_____

_____

5 Minute Weekly
Journaling

_____
_____
_____
_____
_____
_____
_____
_____
_____
_____
_____
_____
_____
_____
_____
_____
_____

5 Minute Weekly
Journaling

_____

_____

_____

_____

_____

_____

_____

_____

_____

_____

_____

_____

_____

_____

_____

Tips: Save for closing costs. Start a home maintenance fund for upkeep and repairs. The better your credit score, the better your interest rates will be.
Buying a home is an investment, keep in mind the future value opportunities of the home.

$	$	$	$	$	$
$	$	$	$	$	$
$	$	$	$	$	$
$	$	$	$	$	$
$	$	$	$	$	$

My MONTHLY ✳ PLAN

May: _____

To do list

_____

_____

_____

_____

_____

Morning Routine

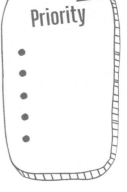

Priority

- ●
- ●
- ●
- ●
- ●

Notes

I love my self

HABIT TRACKER

Name _____
Year _____
Month _____

Habit _____
Goal _____
Done _____
Reward _____

Sun	Mon	Tue	Wed	Thu	Fri	Sat
☐	☐	☐	☐	☐	☐	☐
☐	☐	☐	☐	☐	☐	☐
☐	☐	☐	☐	☐	☐	☐
☐	☐	☐	☐	☐	☐	☐

Habit _____
Goal _____
Done _____
Reward _____

Sun	Mon	Tue	Wed	Thu	Fri	Sat
☐	☐	☐	☐	☐	☐	☐
☐	☐	☐	☐	☐	☐	☐
☐	☐	☐	☐	☐	☐	☐
☐	☐	☐	☐	☐	☐	☐

Habit _____
Goal _____
Done _____
Reward _____

Sun	Mon	Tue	Wed	Thu	Fri	Sat
☐	☐	☐	☐	☐	☐	☐
☐	☐	☐	☐	☐	☐	☐
☐	☐	☐	☐	☐	☐	☐
☐	☐	☐	☐	☐	☐	☐

Habit _____
Goal _____
Done _____
Reward _____

Sun	Mon	Tue	Wed	Thu	Fri	Sat
☐	☐	☐	☐	☐	☐	☐
☐	☐	☐	☐	☐	☐	☐
☐	☐	☐	☐	☐	☐	☐
☐	☐	☐	☐	☐	☐	☐

My Monthly Brain Dump List

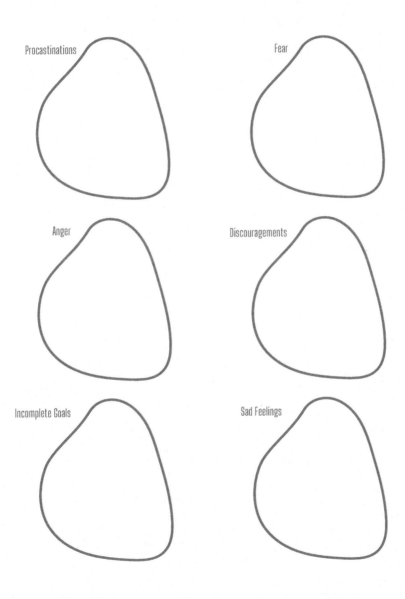

Procastinations

Fear

Anger

Discouragements

Incomplete Goals

Sad Feelings

5 Minute Weekly
Journaling

_____
_____
_____
_____
_____
_____
_____
_____
_____
_____
_____
_____
_____
_____
_____
_____

5 Minute Weekly
Journaling

_____

_____

_____

_____

_____

_____

_____

_____

_____

_____

_____

_____

_____

_____

5 Minute Weekly
Journaling

_____

_____

_____

_____

_____

_____

_____

_____

_____

_____

_____

_____

_____

_____

_____

_____

5 Minute Weekly
Journaling

_____

_____

_____

_____

_____

_____

_____

_____

_____

_____

_____

_____

_____

_____

_____

LIFE/WORK BALANCE

What skills can I use to
increase my income?

What will I do for myself
to maintain a life balance?

What opportunities for growth
are available to me?

Ideal retirement age?
What do I need to do to
accomplish that goal?

Can I improve my
budget to better
meet my goals?

My MONTHLY PLAN

June: _____

To do list

_____
_____
_____
_____
_____

Morning Routine

Priority

-
-
-
-
-

Notes

I love my self

HABIT TRACKER

Name _____
Year _____
Month _____

Habit _____
Goal _____
Done _____
Reward _____

Sun	Mon	Tue	Wed	Thu	Fri	Sat
☐	☐	☐	☐	☐	☐	☐
☐	☐	☐	☐	☐	☐	☐
☐	☐	☐	☐	☐	☐	☐
☐	☐	☐	☐	☐	☐	☐

Habit _____
Goal _____
Done _____
Reward _____

Sun	Mon	Tue	Wed	Thu	Fri	Sat
☐	☐	☐	☐	☐	☐	☐
☐	☐	☐	☐	☐	☐	☐
☐	☐	☐	☐	☐	☐	☐
☐	☐	☐	☐	☐	☐	☐

Habit _____
Goal _____
Done _____
Reward _____

Sun	Mon	Tue	Wed	Thu	Fri	Sat
☐	☐	☐	☐	☐	☐	☐
☐	☐	☐	☐	☐	☐	☐
☐	☐	☐	☐	☐	☐	☐
☐	☐	☐	☐	☐	☐	☐

Habit _____
Goal _____
Done _____
Reward _____

Sun	Mon	Tue	Wed	Thu	Fri	Sat
☐	☐	☐	☐	☐	☐	☐
☐	☐	☐	☐	☐	☐	☐
☐	☐	☐	☐	☐	☐	☐
☐	☐	☐	☐	☐	☐	☐

My Monthly Brain Dump List

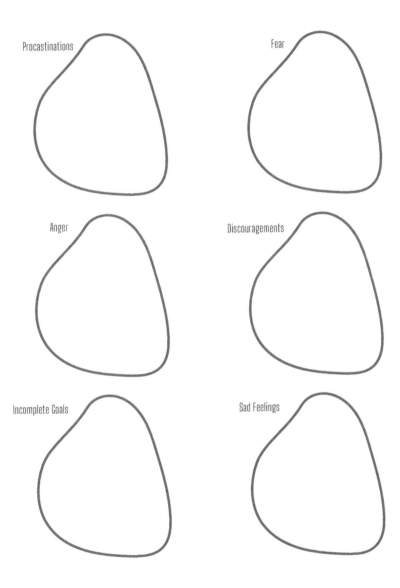

Procastinations

Fear

Anger

Discouragements

Incomplete Goals

Sad Feelings

5 Minute Weekly
Journaling

_____

_____

_____

_____

_____

_____

_____

_____

_____

_____

_____

_____

_____

_____

_____

_____

5 Minute Weekly
Journaling

_____

_____

_____

_____

_____

_____

_____

_____

_____

_____

_____

_____

_____

_____

_____

_____

5 Minute Weekly
Journaling

_____

_____

_____

_____

_____

_____

_____

_____

_____

_____

_____

_____

_____

_____

_____

_____

5 Minute Weekly
Journaling

Quarterly Budget Planner

July, Aug, Sept. _____

INCOME STREAMS

SOURCE	AFTER TAX	ACTUAL	DIFFERENCES
Income			
Side Hustles			
Business			
Others			

FIXED AND VARIABLE EXPENSES

EXPENSES	CURRENT MONTHLY COST	ADJUSTMENTS	MONTHLY DUE DATE
HOUSEHOLD			
RENT/MORTGAGE			
ELECTRIC/GAS/OIL/PROPANE			
WATER/SEWER/SEPTIC/GARBAGE			
RENTER/HOME OWNER INS			
HOME MAINTENANCE			
CAR/MAINTENANCE			
CAR LOAN			
CAR INSURANCE			
CAR MAINTENANCE			
GROCERIES			
FOOD			
HOUSEHOLD ITEMS			
ENTERTAINMENT			
WEEKEND FUN			
WEEKDAY FUN			

Quarterly Budget Planner

HAIR/NAILS			
LAUNDRY			
LUNCH OUT			
PARKING			
GYM/HEALTH CLUB MEMBERSHIP			
INTERNET/CABLE			
STREAMING SUBSCRIPTIONS			
STUDENT LOANS			
TAXES (SELF-EMPLOYED)			
SPORTS/ACTIVITIES			

EXPENSES	CURRENT MONTHLY COST	ADJUSTMENTS	MONTHLY DUE DATE
CHILD CARE			
CLOTHING			
VACATION/TRAVEL			
PROFESSIONAL MEMBERSHIPS			
RX/DR. COPAYS/DENTAL			
HOLIDAYS/BIRTHDAYS			
DEBTS:			

SAVINGS

	TOTAL SAVINGS
Total Income (After Tax)	
Total Fixed Expenses	
Total Variable Expenses	
Savings - Income + Expenses	

COMPOSE A DAILY AFFIRMATION

LIST SIX THINGS YOU WANT SOMEONE TO SAY TO YOU

WHAT MAKES YOU FEEL LOVED AND SAFE?

COMPOSE YOUR AFFIRMATION

My MONTHLY PLAN ✳

July: _____

To do list

_____
_____
_____
_____
_____

Morning Routine

Notes

I love my self

Priority

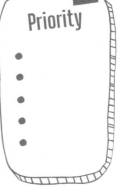

HABIT TRACKER

Name _____
Year _____
Month _____

Habit _____
Goal _____
Done _____
Reward _____

Sun	Mon	Tue	Wed	Thu	Fri	Sat
☐	☐	☐	☐	☐	☐	☐
☐	☐	☐	☐	☐	☐	☐
☐	☐	☐	☐	☐	☐	☐
☐	☐	☐	☐	☐	☐	☐

Habit _____
Goal _____
Done _____
Reward _____

Sun	Mon	Tue	Wed	Thu	Fri	Sat
☐	☐	☐	☐	☐	☐	☐
☐	☐	☐	☐	☐	☐	☐
☐	☐	☐	☐	☐	☐	☐
☐	☐	☐	☐	☐	☐	☐

Habit _____
Goal _____
Done _____
Reward _____

Sun	Mon	Tue	Wed	Thu	Fri	Sat
☐	☐	☐	☐	☐	☐	☐
☐	☐	☐	☐	☐	☐	☐
☐	☐	☐	☐	☐	☐	☐
☐	☐	☐	☐	☐	☐	☐

Habit _____
Goal _____
Done _____
Reward _____

Sun	Mon	Tue	Wed	Thu	Fri	Sat
☐	☐	☐	☐	☐	☐	☐
☐	☐	☐	☐	☐	☐	☐
☐	☐	☐	☐	☐	☐	☐
☐	☐	☐	☐	☐	☐	☐

My Monthly Brain Dump List

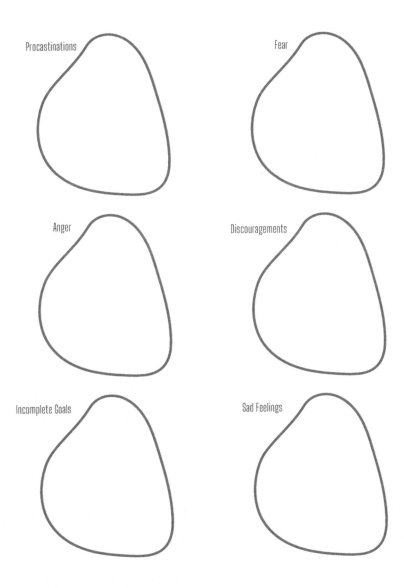

Procastinations

Fear

Anger

Discouragements

Incomplete Goals

Sad Feelings

5 Minute Weekly
Journaling

_____
_____
_____
_____
_____
_____
_____
_____
_____
_____
_____
_____
_____
_____
_____
_____

5 Minute Weekly
Journaling

_____

_____

_____

_____

_____

_____

_____

_____

_____

_____

_____

_____

_____

_____

_____

5 Minute Weekly
Journaling

_____

_____

_____

_____

_____

_____

_____

_____

_____

_____

_____

_____

_____

_____

_____

_____

_____

5 Minute Weekly
Journaling

_____

_____

_____

_____

_____

_____

_____

_____

_____

_____

_____

_____

_____

_____

_____

_____

_____

Having a variety of credit types (i.e. car, home, credit card, loan) helps show credibility

The better your credit score, the lower your interest rates on borrowed credit will be.

Build trust with banks and creditors by paying on time.

Keep credit card balances below 50% of credit limit.

How Do I Build My Credit Score?

Only use your credit card for things in your budget to ensure you pay it off each month.

If you agree to co-sign for someone, be prepared to pay the full amount if they default on payments.

Use a secured credit card to build credit.

Paying the minimums on cards only pays for the interest. Pay more to pay it off.

My MONTHLY PLAN

August:
_____

Morning Routine

To do list

_____

_____

_____

_____

_____

Priority

- ●
- ●
- ●
- ●
- ●

Notes

I love my self

HABIT TRACKER

Name _____
Year _____
Month _____

	Sun	Mon	Tue	Wed	Thu	Fri	Sat

Habit _____
Goal _____
Done _____
Reward _____

	Sun	Mon	Tue	Wed	Thu	Fri	Sat

Habit _____
Goal _____
Done _____
Reward _____

	Sun	Mon	Tue	Wed	Thu	Fri	Sat

Habit _____
Goal _____
Done _____
Reward _____

	Sun	Mon	Tue	Wed	Thu	Fri	Sat

Habit _____
Goal _____
Done _____
Reward _____

My Monthly Brain Dump List

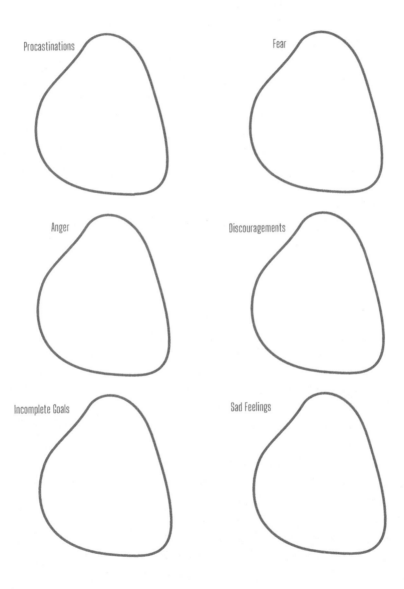

Procastinations

Fear

Anger

Discouragements

Incomplete Goals

Sad Feelings

5 Minute Weekly
Journaling

_____

_____

_____

_____

_____

_____

_____

_____

_____

_____

_____

_____

_____

_____

_____

_____

_____

_____

5 Minute Weekly Journaling

_____
_____
_____
_____
_____
_____
_____
_____
_____
_____
_____
_____
_____
_____
_____
_____

5 Minute Weekly
Journaling

_____

_____

_____

_____

_____

_____

_____

_____

_____

_____

_____

_____

_____

_____

_____

_____

_____

5 Minute Weekly
Journaling

_____

_____

_____

_____

_____

_____

_____

_____

_____

_____

_____

_____

_____

_____

_____

_____

HOLIDAY/EVENT
BUDGET

*Pay yourself bi-weekly
in a savings account.

Holiday Budget Goal	Event Budget Goal

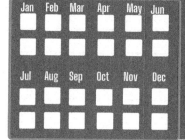

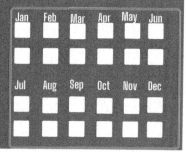

My MONTHLY ✳ PLAN

September: _____

To do list

_____

_____

_____

_____

_____

Morning Routine

Priority

- •
- •
- •
- •
- •

Notes

I love my self

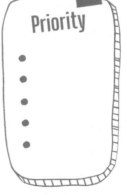

HABIT TRACKER

Name _____
Year _____
Month _____

Habit _____
Goal _____
Done _____
Reward _____

Sun	Mon	Tue	Wed	Thu	Fri	Sat
☐	☐	☐	☐	☐	☐	☐
☐	☐	☐	☐	☐	☐	☐
☐	☐	☐	☐	☐	☐	☐
☐	☐	☐	☐	☐	☐	☐

Habit _____
Goal _____
Done _____
Reward _____

Sun	Mon	Tue	Wed	Thu	Fri	Sat
☐	☐	☐	☐	☐	☐	☐
☐	☐	☐	☐	☐	☐	☐
☐	☐	☐	☐	☐	☐	☐
☐	☐	☐	☐	☐	☐	☐

Habit _____
Goal _____
Done _____
Reward _____

Sun	Mon	Tue	Wed	Thu	Fri	Sat
☐	☐	☐	☐	☐	☐	☐
☐	☐	☐	☐	☐	☐	☐
☐	☐	☐	☐	☐	☐	☐
☐	☐	☐	☐	☐	☐	☐

Habit _____
Goal _____
Done _____
Reward _____

Sun	Mon	Tue	Wed	Thu	Fri	Sat
☐	☐	☐	☐	☐	☐	☐
☐	☐	☐	☐	☐	☐	☐
☐	☐	☐	☐	☐	☐	☐
☐	☐	☐	☐	☐	☐	☐

My Monthly Brain Dump List

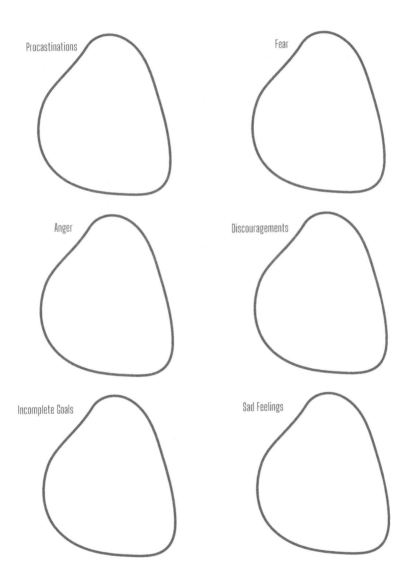

Procastinations

Fear

Anger

Discouragements

Incomplete Goals

Sad Feelings

5 Minute Weekly
Journaling

_____

_____

_____

_____

_____

_____

_____

_____

_____

_____

_____

_____

_____

_____

_____

_____

5 Minute Weekly
Journaling

_____
_____
_____
_____
_____
_____
_____
_____
_____
_____
_____
_____
_____
_____
_____
_____
_____

5 Minute Weekly Journaling

_____
_____
_____
_____
_____
_____
_____
_____
_____
_____
_____
_____
_____
_____
_____
_____

5 Minute Weekly Journaling

_____

_____

_____

_____

_____

_____

_____

_____

_____

_____

_____

_____

_____

_____

_____

_____

Quarterly Budget Planner

Oct, Nov, Dec. _____

INCOME STREAMS

SOURCE	AFTER TAX	ACTUAL	DIFFERENCES
Income			
Side Hustles			
Business			
Others			

FIXED AND VARIABLE EXPENSES

EXPENSES	CURRENT MONTHLY COST	ADJUSTMENTS	MONTHLY DUE DATE
HOUSEHOLD			
RENT/MORTGAGE			
ELECTRIC/GAS/OIL/PROPANE			
WATER/SEWER/SEPTIC/GARBAGE			
RENTER/HOME OWNER INS			
HOME MAINTENANCE			
CAR/MAINTENANCE			
CAR LOAN			
CAR INSURANCE			
CAR MAINTENANCE			
GROCERIES			
FOOD			
HOUSEHOLD ITEMS			
ENTERTAINMENT			
WEEKEND FUN			
WEEKDAY FUN			

Quarterly Budget Planner

HAIR/NAILS			
LAUNDRY			
LUNCH OUT			
PARKING			
GYM/HEALTH CLUB MEMBERSHIP			
INTERNET/CABLE			
STREAMING SUBSCRIPTIONS			
STUDENT LOANS			
TAXES (SELF-EMPLOYED)			
SPORTS/ACTIVITIES			

EXPENSES	CURRENT MONTHLY COST	ADJUSTMENTS	MONTHLY DUE DATE
CHILD CARE			
CLOTHING			
VACATION/TRAVEL			
PROFESSIONAL MEMBERSHIPS			
RX/DR. COPAYS/DENTAL			
HOLIDAYS/BIRTHDAYS			
DEBTS:			

SAVINGS

	TOTAL SAVINGS
Total Income (After Tax)	
Total Fixed Expenses	
Total Variable Expenses	
Savings - Income + Expenses	

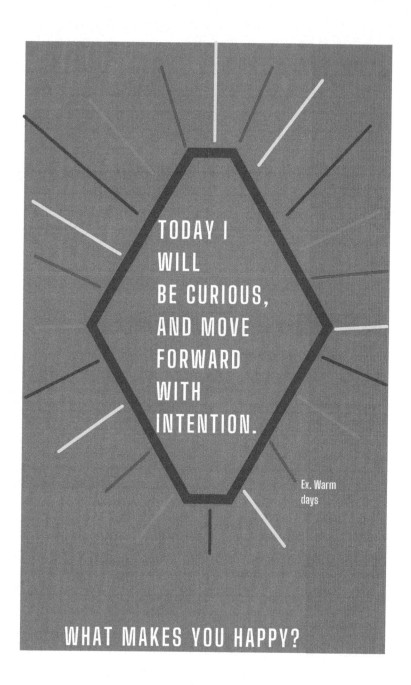

TODAY I
WILL
BE CURIOUS,
AND MOVE
FORWARD
WITH
INTENTION.

Ex. Warm
days

WHAT MAKES YOU HAPPY?

My MONTHLY PLAN

October: _____

To do list

_____

_____

_____

_____

_____

Morning Routine

Priority

-
-
-
-
-

Notes

I love my self

HABIT TRACKER

Name _____
Year _____
Month _____

Sun	Mon	Tue	Wed	Thu	Fri	Sat

Habit _____
Goal _____
Done _____
Reward _____

Sun	Mon	Tue	Wed	Thu	Fri	Sat

Habit _____
Goal _____
Done _____
Reward _____

Sun	Mon	Tue	Wed	Thu	Fri	Sat

Habit _____
Goal _____
Done _____
Reward _____

Sun	Mon	Tue	Wed	Thu	Fri	Sat

Habit _____
Goal _____
Done _____
Reward _____

Sun	Mon	Tue	Wed	Thu	Fri	Sat

My Monthly Brain Dump List

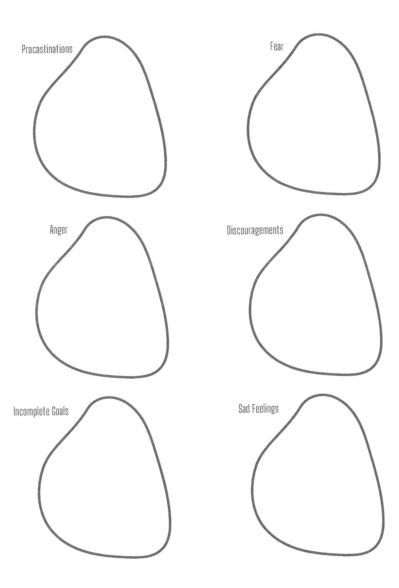

Procastinations

Fear

Anger

Discouragements

Incomplete Goals

Sad Feelings

5 Minute Weekly Journaling

_____

_____

_____

_____

_____

_____

_____

_____

_____

_____

_____

_____

_____

_____

_____

_____

5 Minute Weekly
Journaling

_____

_____

_____

_____

_____

_____

_____

_____

_____

_____

_____

_____

_____

_____

_____

5 Minute Weekly
Journaling

_____

_____

_____

_____

_____

_____

_____

_____

_____

_____

_____

_____

_____

_____

_____

_____

5 Minute Weekly
Journaling

_____
_____
_____
_____
_____
_____
_____
_____
_____
_____
_____
_____
_____
_____
_____
_____

Emergency Fund Goal

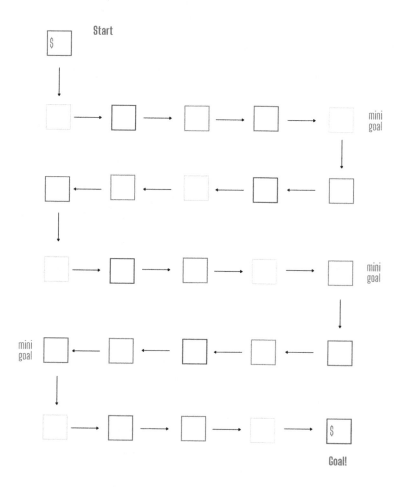

Start

mini goal

mini goal

mini goal

$ **Goal!**

Emergency funds are for unexpected costs. Loss of a job, medical bills, car or home repairs. It is best to keep three months of expenses saved aside. I need to save: $

My MONTHLY ✱
PLAN

November: _____

To do list

_____
_____
_____
_____

Morning Routine

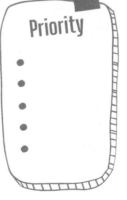

Priority

- •
- •
- •
- •
- •

Notes

I love my self

HABIT TRACKER

Name _____
Year _____
Month _____

		Sun	Mon	Tue	Wed	Thu	Fri	Sat
Habit	_____	☐	☐	☐	☐	☐	☐	☐
Goal	_____	☐	☐	☐	☐	☐	☐	☐
Done	_____	☐	☐	☐	☐	☐	☐	☐
Reward	_____	☐	☐	☐	☐	☐	☐	☐

		Sun	Mon	Tue	Wed	Thu	Fri	Sat
Habit	_____	☐	☐	☐	☐	☐	☐	☐
Goal	_____	☐	☐	☐	☐	☐	☐	☐
Done	_____	☐	☐	☐	☐	☐	☐	☐
Reward	_____	☐	☐	☐	☐	☐	☐	☐

		Sun	Mon	Tue	Wed	Thu	Fri	Sat
Habit	_____	☐	☐	☐	☐	☐	☐	☐
Goal	_____	☐	☐	☐	☐	☐	☐	☐
Done	_____	☐	☐	☐	☐	☐	☐	☐
Reward	_____	☐	☐	☐	☐	☐	☐	☐

		Sun	Mon	Tue	Wed	Thu	Fri	Sat
Habit	_____	☐	☐	☐	☐	☐	☐	☐
Goal	_____	☐	☐	☐	☐	☐	☐	☐
Done	_____	☐	☐	☐	☐	☐	☐	☐
Reward	_____	☐	☐	☐	☐	☐	☐	☐

My Monthly Brain Dump List

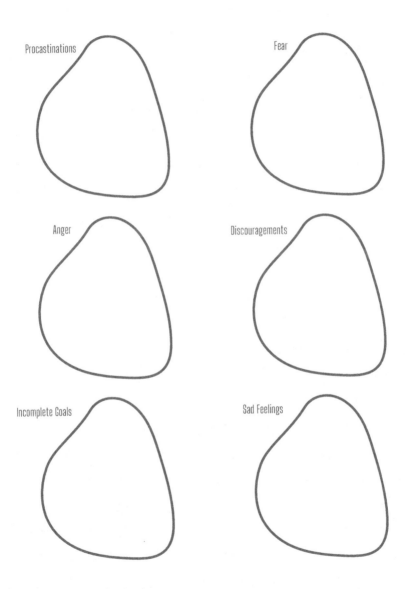

Procastinations

Fear

Anger

Discouragements

Incomplete Goals

Sad Feelings

5 Minute Weekly Journaling

_____

_____

_____

_____

_____

_____

_____

_____

_____

_____

_____

_____

_____

_____

_____

_____

5 Minute Weekly
Journaling

_____

_____

_____

_____

_____

_____

_____

_____

_____

_____

_____

_____

_____

_____

_____

_____

5 Minute Weekly
Journaling

_____

_____

_____

_____

_____

_____

_____

_____

_____

_____

_____

_____

_____

_____

_____

_____

_____

5 Minute Weekly
Journaling

_____

_____

_____

_____

_____

_____

_____

_____

_____

_____

_____

_____

_____

_____

_____

_____

Things to Remember

Your wants and needs are valid

Productivity doesn't define your worth.

Your boundaries are important and worth respect.

Your mistakes don't define you.

Taking time for yourself is NOT selfish.

It is okay to ask for help. Communities exist for our growth through support.

My MONTHLY PLAN ✳

December: _____

To do list

_____
_____
_____
_____
_____

Morning Routine

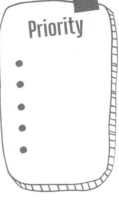

Priority

- •
- •
- •
- •
- •

Notes

I love my self

HABIT TRACKER

Name _____
Year _____
Month _____

Habit _____
Goal _____
Done _____
Reward _____

Sun	Mon	Tue	Wed	Thu	Fri	Sat
☐	☐	☐	☐	☐	☐	☐
☐	☐	☐	☐	☐	☐	☐
☐	☐	☐	☐	☐	☐	☐
☐	☐	☐	☐	☐	☐	☐

Habit _____
Goal _____
Done _____
Reward _____

Sun	Mon	Tue	Wed	Thu	Fri	Sat
☐	☐	☐	☐	☐	☐	☐
☐	☐	☐	☐	☐	☐	☐
☐	☐	☐	☐	☐	☐	☐
☐	☐	☐	☐	☐	☐	☐

Habit _____
Goal _____
Done _____
Reward _____

Sun	Mon	Tue	Wed	Thu	Fri	Sat
☐	☐	☐	☐	☐	☐	☐
☐	☐	☐	☐	☐	☐	☐
☐	☐	☐	☐	☐	☐	☐
☐	☐	☐	☐	☐	☐	☐

Habit _____
Goal _____
Done _____
Reward _____

Sun	Mon	Tue	Wed	Thu	Fri	Sat
☐	☐	☐	☐	☐	☐	☐
☐	☐	☐	☐	☐	☐	☐
☐	☐	☐	☐	☐	☐	☐
☐	☐	☐	☐	☐	☐	☐

My Monthly Brain Dump List

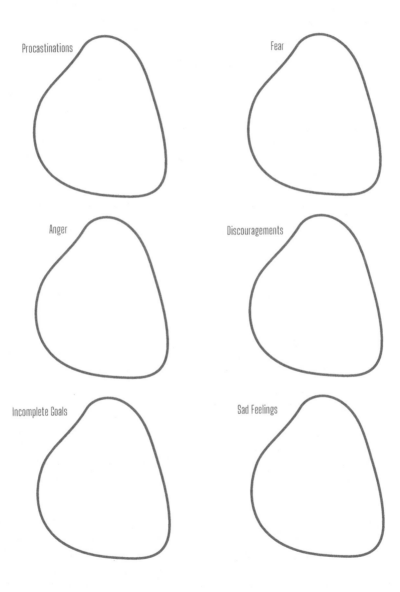

Procastinations

Fear

Anger

Discouragements

Incomplete Goals

Sad Feelings

5 Minute Weekly
Journaling

_____

_____

_____

_____

_____

_____

_____

_____

_____

_____

_____

_____

_____

_____

_____

_____

5 Minute Weekly
Journaling

---

5 Minute Weekly
Journaling

_____
_____
_____
_____
_____
_____
_____
_____
_____
_____
_____
_____
_____
_____
_____
_____
_____

5 Minute Weekly
Journaling

_____
_____
_____
_____
_____
_____
_____
_____
_____
_____
_____
_____
_____
_____
_____
_____
_____
_____

Made in the USA
Columbia, SC
30 June 2022

62449855R00065